THE EXPEDITIONS OF
CORTES

Nigel Hunter

Illustrated by Peter Bull

The Bookwright Press
New York · 1990

Great Journeys

Cover *Hernán Cortés led his army through many battles to conquer the Aztec capital, Tenochtitlán.*

Frontispiece *This portrait of Hernán Cortés shows him at the height of his power and fame.*

J.92
910.92
HUN

First published in the
United States in 1990 by
The Bookwright Press
387 Park Avenue South
New York, NY 10016

First published in 1990 by
Wayland (Publishers) Limited
61 Western Road, Hove
East Sussex, BN3 1JD, England

© Copyright 1990 Wayland (Publishers) Limited

Typeset by DP Press Ltd, Sevenoaks, England
Printed in Italy by G. Canale & C.S.p.A., Turin

Hunter, Nigel.
   Hernán Cortés / by Nigel Hunter.
   32 p. cm. — (Great journeys)
   Bibliography: p.
   Includes index.
   Summary: An account of Cortés' life as an adventurer which culminated in his conquest and domination of the Aztec civiliza in Mexico.
   ISBN 0–531–18335–1
   1. Cortés, Hernán, 1485–1547—Juvenile literature. 2. Mexic History—Conquest, 1519–1540—Juvenile literature. 3. Explor 4. Mexico—History—Conquest, 1519–1540. [1. Cortéz, Herna 1485–1547.]   I. Title.   II. Series.
F1230.C835H86   1990
[92]—dc20   89–17

Contents

A Soldier of Spain

Tenochtitlán, the Aztec capital, was the most beautiful city in the world, said Hernán Cortés. Not long afterward, amid scenes of appalling slaughter, he gave orders to destroy it.

On its ruins a new capital was built, Mexico City. Catholic churches now stand where once there were Aztec temples. In the church of the Hospital of Jesus, a national monument, lie the bones of Hernán Cortés, the Spanish *conquistador*.

In museums lie remnants of the ancient civilizations of Central America – the Mayans, the Olmecs and Mixtecs; the Totonacs and Toltecs; and the doomed Mexica, otherwise known as the Aztecs.

At many sites, impressive evidence of these former cultures can be seen, such as stepped pyramids that rival in splendor the pyramids of Egypt. The largest of these was built at Cholula between AD 300 and AD 900. It was dedicated to the god Quetzalcóatl (which means Feathered Serpent).

When Cortés landed on the Yucatán coast in AD 1519, he was believed by many of the native people to be Quetzalcóatl himself, returning to reclaim his land after centuries of exile. Montezuma, the Aztec ruler,

Above *Cortés as he may have appeared around the time of his earliest conquests.*

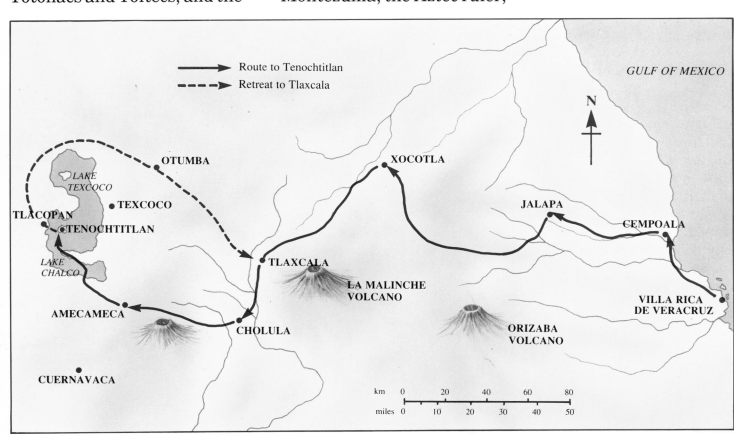

Left *The ruins of an Aztec city in the Yucatán peninsula in Mexico.*

was among those who thought this was possible: the god's return had been foretold in legend.

Cortés, who is a significant figure in the history of Spain, lived in an exciting period of exploration and discovery. He was born in the town of Medellín, in the rugged, inhospitable region of Extremadura, in 1485. From his father, a former soldier, he must have heard many exciting tales of military deeds.

For centuries, Spain had been dominated by the Moors of North Africa; but Christian forces were succeeding in claiming the country. In 1492, Granada, the last stronghold of the Muslim invaders, was overthrown. Spain was united as a Christian nation.

1492 was also the year of Christopher Columbus's attempt to find a westward route to the far east. While trying to prove that the world was round, Columbus came upon some islands previously unknown to Europeans. He assumed they lay off the coast of Asia. The islands were referred to as the Indies, and their people were called "Indians." In fact, Columbus had arrived at Watling Island, in the heart of the Bahamas.

Before long, a Spanish settlement was founded on the island of Hispaniola. Then in 1502, the Florentine navigator Amerigo Vespucci charted thousands of miles of coastline to the west, and the New World gained its present-day name of America.

Cortés was a young man of some learning. He was also high-spirited and restless. Reports from the Indies suggested many opportunities for excitement and adventure; he decided to make the voyage to the New World himself.

Far left *This map shows the route Cortés took on his journey to Tenochtitlán and his retreat to Tlaxcala.*

The Indies

Cortés sailed in 1504 as a passenger on a merchant ship taking supplies to Hispaniola. It was an eventful voyage.

Off the Canary Islands, the ship's mainmast was toppled by a fierce storm. This meant a struggle into port and a delay for repairs. Then, much farther into the crossing, the captain lost his way. Food supplies were getting low. Rainwater had to be gathered from the sails and stored for drinking. But then one day a dove was sighted on top of the rigging. The ship changed course to follow as the bird flew on, and soon, to everyone's relief, the port of Santo Domingo was reached.

On arrival, Cortés was given land and local people to work it. He hoped, as others did, that gold might be found; but he had no such luck. Cortés remained in Hispaniola for seven years, becoming chief legal officer in the town of Azúa. He also became close to Diego Velázquez, the island's most prominent citizen.

In 1511, Velázquez was chosen to lead an expedition to Cuba, and Cortés had no hesitation in joining him. He proved a brave and skillful fighter. The people of Cuba were soon defeated. Once the Spanish had established their hold on the island, Cortés was

Above *Diego Velázquez, governor of Cuba. He was at one time a friend of Cortés, but was later to become his life-long enemy.*

Left *A small Spanish sailing ship of the kind used in early exploration of the American coast.*

Right Cortés leaving Mexico in 1519. Despite this seemingly friendly farewell to Velázquez, there were strong underlying tensions between them.

Below The coast of Yucatán, gateway to the Aztec empire.

appointed secretary to Governor Velázquez.

Another seven years passed. In Cuba, Cortés grew increasingly influential and wise to the ways of the world. He learned that he sometimes needed to use cunning in order to further his career.

He became involved in a plot against Velázquez, which was discovered. He was imprisoned, but managed to escape; then he was caught again, yet for a second time, he got away. Eventually, Cortés and Velázquez settled their quarrel. It had arisen partly from personal matters that were resolved by Cortés' marriage to a young Spanish woman, Catalina Juárez.

By now, Cortés was chief magistrate at Santiago. His Cuban estate not only brought wealth from cattle and sheep-farming, it also yielded considerable quantities of gold. However, his ambition for yet more power burned as strongly as ever.

Then in 1517 an expedition returned to Cuba from the coast of Yucatán, the eastern peninsula of Mexico. The returning adventurers brought back precious objects made of gold that had been stolen from the local temples. Their many injuries showed that the people of the mainland could be dangerous enemies.

After two further expeditions failed to return on schedule, Velázquez asked Cortés to lead another mission. Cortés was more than willing; he knew this was the chance he had been waiting for. If he succeeded he would find his fortune.

Conquistadores

Cortés put all his wealth into the expedition. He also borrowed a great deal of money. Most of the money was spent on ships, eleven in all. They were mainly small open-decked vessels, but the flagship was a 100-ton caravel.

Food supplies consisted mostly of bread, flour, beans and meat (with live chickens and pigs taken on board). To drink, there was wine and water, stored in kegs. Cortés also gathered a store of cheap articles such as glass beads, small mirrors, belt-buckles and scissors to barter with the local people for valuables. However, this was clearly a military expedition.

The weapon supplies included crossbows, muskets and cannon, together with the necessary arrows, gunpowder and shot, plus swords, and steel-tipped javelins and lances. Cortés also bought sixteen horses.

The horses, which were previously unknown on the mainland, were to prove invaluable in battle. The local people were terrified of them and, at first, thought a horse and rider to be some kind of supernatural beast.

Eventually Cortés gathered 550 soldiers together, all hoping for riches and sure of the justice of their cause. "We are engaging in a just and good war which will bring us fame," he announced to them all, shortly before sailing. "Almighty God, in whose name

Above *Cortés loaded his ships with enough supplies for a long and hard campaign.*

and faith it is waged, will assuredly give us victory."

The fleet left Cuba in February 1519. The first part of Yucatán reached was an island called Cozumel. The people there offered the *conquistadores* no resistance. Meekly, they allowed the idols in their temples to be broken up and replaced by crosses and a shrine. Christian conversion was one of the main aims of the Spanish; they considered the local religions to be an evil form of witchcraft.

The expedition's Indian interpreter was replaced by a Spanish sailor who had been shipwrecked years before and held as a slave on the mainland. Sought out by a messenger from Cortés, he was released on the payment of a few glass beads to join his comrades as they set off around the coast.

The first fighting took place near the town of Tabasco. Lasting several days, it ended in a battle that involved as many as 40,000 local warriors. Only then did Cortés order his horsemen into action. The cavalry proved decisive. The Indians counted their dead in hundreds, while the Spanish lost no more than forty men.

The Indians gave Cortés twenty local women. Among them was a beautiful girl whom they christened Marina. Her close relationship with Cortés was to be extremely important in the future.

Below *The Spanish horsemen wrought havoc among their Indian enemies.*

A Distant Kingdom

The defeated people of Tabasco had little gold to give the *conquistadores*. However, they told of a great civilization to the west – the Aztec empire, which was rich in gold and precious stones. It was the first time that the Spanish had heard of the Aztecs. This information encouraged them to continue their journey.

They sailed farther along the coast to San Juan de Alúa, a point first reached by an earlier expedition from Cuba. Here they were welcomed by the local people. The Indians brought the Spanish vast amounts of food, such as smoked fish, whole roast turkeys, tortillas and fruit, and helped them to set up camp.

Then there were ceremonial exchanges of gifts. Cortés received many beautifully made items among which were a serpent's-head mask of turquoise mosaic, a feathered headdress, a jade necklace and

Below *This engraving, made 200 years after the conquest of Mexico, shows the Great Temple at Tenochtitlán. Human sacrifices are being flung down the steps.*

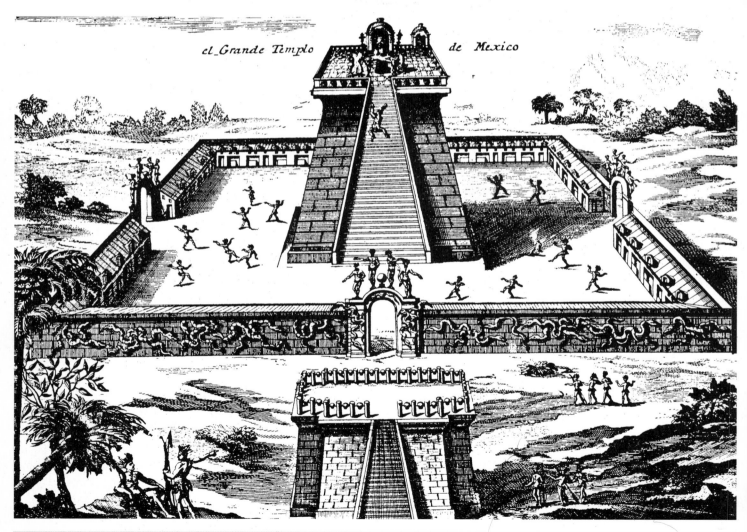

el Grande Templo de Mexico

__Above__ An ornamental turquoise mask that could possibly be one of the gifts given to Cortés by Montezuma.

of silver, representing the moon, and one of gold, representing the sun. But Montezuma refused to meet Cortés.

For the previous ten years, the Aztec ruler had lived in dread of strangers. His empire was founded on the blood of human sacrifice. To satisfy the great god Huitzilopochtli (Left-handed Hummingbird) who was god of war and of the sun, tens of thousands of people were sacrificed each year.

However, Quetzalcóatl, a powerful god of ancient times, had disapproved of human sacrifice. According to the legend telling of his defeat, Quetzalcóatl sailed away on a raft of snakes. He vowed that he would return from the east on his own name-day. This, it was said, would herald the end of the Aztec nation.

Then, in the years before the Spanish arrived, many strange omens were seen, including a three-tailed comet that blazed in the sky for forty nights. There were reports of a speaking rock, which foretold doom and split into pieces, and a strange bird with a mirror set into its neck.

Looking into the bird's mirror, the Aztec emperor saw men in unfamiliar clothes, marching and fighting; some rode monstrous deer-like creatures. Then, on the very day appointed by the god for his return, Cortés and his men landed. And, like ancient pictures of Quetzalcóatl, Cortés was noticeably pale-skinned. Very quickly, Montezuma was becoming a worried man.

a shield studded with gold. The Spanish adventurers had reached the outer regions of the Aztec empire.

For the first time, they heard the name of the Aztec emperor, Montezuma. Cortés made it clear that he wanted to meet Montezuma, saying that the Spanish came as friends. Messages and gifts were sent inland to the Aztec capital, Tenochtitlán.

Montezuma sent Cortés splendid gifts in return. These included two enormous, weighty disks; these were calendars, one

Allies

Before moving on, Cortés acted deviously to free himself from his loyalty to Velázquez. He intended to become governor of this new territory himself.

He resigned as the expedition's leader and promptly formed a "town council," with himself as Captain-General and Chief Justice. Then he sent a ship to seek a suitable site for the town itself. He already had a name for it: Villa Rica de Vera Cruz.

A site was found 25 mi (40 km) to the north. To reach it, the Spaniards marched overland, passing through fertile farmland, skirting forests full of exotic birds and flowers. They were invited to visit Cempoala, the capital of the Totonac people.

The Totonacs were bitterly resentful of Aztec rule. The Aztecs not only demanded material goods from their subjects (foodstuffs, textiles, gold and precious jewels such as jade), they also demanded victims for sacrifice. The Totonacs saw the Spanish as possible allies. Hundreds went with them as porters.

Shortly afterward, there arrived in the region five splendidly dressed Aztec dignitaries who had come to

Below The people of Cempoala welcomed the Spaniards and helped them on their march through the dense Mexican forests.

Above The Totonacs made a formal alliance with the Spanish because of the Aztec demands for sacrificial victims.

claim twenty Totonacs for sacrifice. Cortés seized the chance to form an alliance with the Totonacs on his own terms.

He suggested that the five Aztecs should be taken prisoner, saying he would support the Totonacs in the event of hostilities. Then, that night, Cortés secretly freed two of the captives, sending them to Montezuma with another message of friendship. Their "escape" threw the Totonacs into panic. Expecting an attack at any time, they formally bound themselves to Spain.

Instead of an army, however, Montezuma sent messengers, once again loaded with gifts. He dared not attack, believing the mysterious stranger to be, quite

possibly, a god. Instead, he sought to persuade Cortés, with gifts of treasure, to leave. Cortés sent the envoys back with the three remaining prisoners and a message of his own: he and Montezuma would meet soon.

He also wrote to the Spanish king, Charles I, reporting recent events and future prospects. Cortés took great care to tell the king of his own loyalty and the greed and unreliability of Velázquez.

With his letter, Cortés sent all of the treasure he and his men had so far acquired. This was meant to show Charles what he might expect in the future. The king was due one fifth of the treasure; Cortés was due one fifth of what was left.

Into the Interior

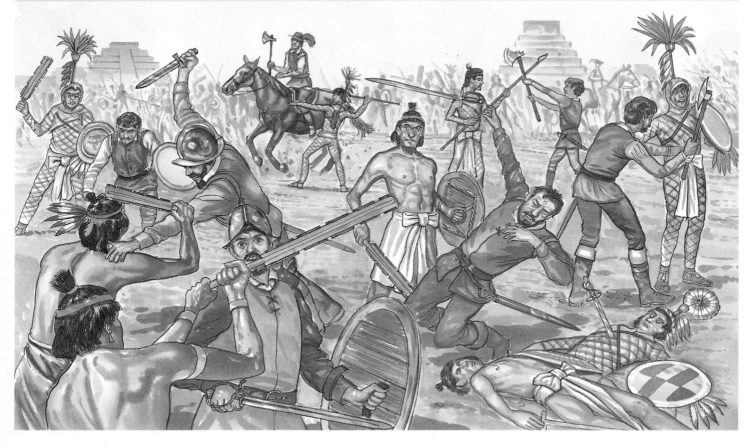

Cortés' decision to march inland to the Aztec capital was accompanied by an order to wreck his fleet. Without the possibility of retreat, Cortés was sure his men would fight all the harder. They set out in August 1519, backed by a thousand Totonac warriors.

It was a tough march, through steaming tropical forests, across dry, barren deserts and over cold, dangerous mountain passes. At one point, they reached a vast stone wall, marking the boundaries of the people of Tlaxcala. Cortés knew that the Tlaxcalans were enemies of the Aztecs, and he hoped to make allies of them.

However, his messages of peace to the Tlaxcalan chiefs were received with deep distrust. He and his men were often ambushed. During one full-scale battle, the body of a fallen horse was seized by the Indians to be cut up and sent around the territory. The pieces of this body were proof that these strange creatures were not supernatural at all.

After three weeks' fighting, with heavy losses on both sides, the Spanish defeated the Tlaxcalans. They were invited into the city, where the people treated them with great

Above *The battle against the Tlaxcalans was the most fierce the Spaniards had yet fought.*

courtesy and respect. As before, the defeated people offered women to the victors. When they were duly baptized, Cortés accepted them.

Meanwhile, Cortés was still receiving envoys with gifts and messages from Montezuma. Still he tried to persuade Cortés to retreat. Then at last it seemed that Montezuma had given in to the inevitable; he invited Cortés to Tenochtitlán.

The way led through Cholula, a city whose people were said to be highly untrustworthy. Their friendly reception did indeed prove treacherous. A few days after entering the city, Cortés learned of a plot. Doña Marina (the slave-girl from Tabasco, to whom he had become closely attached) told Cortés about a conversation she had had with an old woman. The Cholulans, with thousands of Aztecs nearby, were planning to attack.

Cortés took the initiative. The following day, the Spanish and their Tlaxcalan allies killed thousands of Indians in the streets and squares of Cholula. From then on the Cholulans would be bound to Spain.

As the Spanish moved nearer to Tenochtitlán, envoys from Montezuma again tried to persuade them to turn back. But, from the peak of the majestic volcano Popocatépetl, the capital could be seen in the distance. Nothing could stop them now. Cortés would be there in just a few days.

Below The conquistadores *defeated the Cholulans in a surprise attack. After their defeat, like the Tlaxcalans, they became allies of the Spanish.*

The Aztec Capital

Tenochtitlán lay at the center of a vast shimmering lake. Around the shores of the lake were many other cities, some of which were connected to the capital by causeways. As Cortés and his men and their Indian allies advanced, many local people in canoes paddled close to view the meeting. It was November 1519.

The Aztec emperor was carried shoulder-high in a sumptuously decorated carriage down the southern causeway. He was attended by many nobles and courtiers, all in magnificent dress. He greeted Cortés with a stately speech, which was both respectful and welcoming. The Spaniards were given garlands of flowers, and necklaces of gold. Throughout the proceedings, it was Marina who acted as interpreter.

On entering the capital, the Spaniards and their allies were taken to a vast and splendid royal palace, where they were to be lodged in style. Montezuma seemed ready to accept them and obey them as the rightful heirs to his empire. For some time, all was peaceful. The splendors of the city, with its botanical gardens and exotic aviaries and zoos, its markets teeming with produce and its many canals and public squares, much impressed the Spaniards.

However, despite their welcome, the Spaniards felt considerable unease. The blood-soaked pyramid-top temples, with their fearsome statues, were terrible to behold – as was the central city's skull-rack, with its evidence of tens of thousands of sacrificial victims. The victims climbed up the steps of the pyramid to the sacrificial stone, where their hearts were ripped out. The bodies were dismembered and eaten in a cannibal feast.

Then came news that some of the soldiers who had been left to guard Vera Cruz had been attacked, on the orders of Aztec agents. Boldly, Cortés informed

Below At the head of his victorious army, Cortés entered the Aztec capital in splendor.

Montezuma that he was under arrest; from then on, the once proud emperor was forced to live as a hostage in the palace he had given over to Cortés. The offending Aztec agents, summoned back to the capital, were burned alive. Soon afterward, Montezuma swore loyalty, on behalf of his people, to Spain.

Some months passed, during which a great store of treasure was secured by the Spanish. Cortés and Montezuma spent much time in religious discussion, but the human sacrifices continued. Then one day, visiting the main Aztec temple, Cortés lost patience and smashed the statue of the god Huitzilopochtli. A Christian altar was set up in its place.

Day by day, the Aztecs' resentment of the Spanish grew.

Under Attack

In May 1520, Cortés left the Aztec capital to deal with some trouble on the coast. From Cuba, Diego Velázquez had sent a force against him. Cortés took about one hundred soldiers, leaving the remainder in Tenochtitlán under the command of one of his lieutenants, Pedro de Alvarado.

Through a combination of bribery and force, Cortés overcame his opponents. But much worse trouble followed immediately. Word arrived that Alvarado had ordered a massacre within the grounds of the main temple at Tenochtitlán during an Aztec festival. Now the Aztecs were attacking the Spanish in their headquarters. Cortés hurried back, in cold fury. With him went several hundred of the soldiers who had recently arrived from Cuba.

Surprisingly, Tenochtitlán seemed almost deserted. The very next day, however, with all the Spaniards (and their Tlaxcalan allies) together in their royal apartments, the Aztec onslaught began in earnest. Montezuma had been replaced as ruler by his brother, Cuitláhuac.

With stones flung from slingshots, with spears and with a storm of arrows (some on fire so as to set parts of the palace ablaze), the Aztecs attacked. They had sworn to kill, or capture for sacrifice, every Spanish soldier, even at a cost of 20,000 of their own men for each Spaniard's life.

The toll of dead mounted and Cortés himself was badly injured in one hand. An attempted break-out of the city failed. As a desperate measure, Cortés took the captive Montezuma in chains to the palace roof, to try to call off the siege. For the former emperor, this proved fatal; hit by a hail of

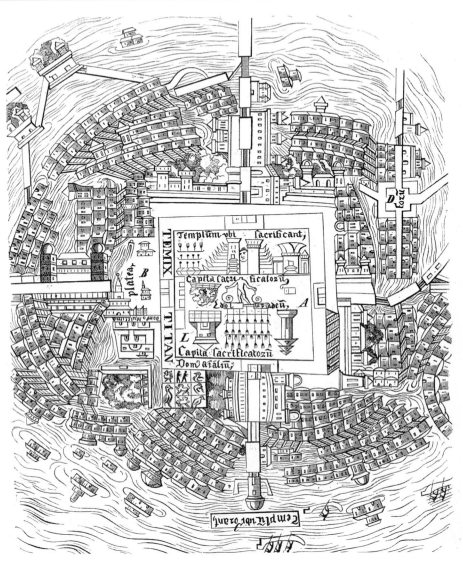

Above A plan of Tenochtitlán drawn for Cortés. At that time, Tenochtitlán was probably the most heavily populated city in the world.

stones, he died of his injuries three days later.

Then Cortés ordered a second break-out attempt, to take place at night. He chose the shortest route, the western causeway, which was linked to the city of Tlacopán. The Spanish took a hastily built portable bridge with them to help cross gaps in the causeways deliberately created by their enemies. But the Aztecs were waiting for them. The war drums and conch-shell trumpets sounded, and in fleets of canoes, the Aztecs attacked.

That night, June 30, 1520, became known as the *Noche Triste* (Sad Night). The Spaniards lost hundreds of men; the Tlaxcalans, thousands. Spanish soldiers who had weighed themselves down with treasure were especially vulnerable. The portable bridge was destroyed at the first gap in the causeway. Other gaps were filled with dead bodies, allowing some soldiers to pass over them, and eventually reach dry land.

The survivors faced still more fighting, including a great battle on the plains near Otumba, in which Cortés showed great tactical skill and courage. But finally, Cortés' forces, weary and weak with hunger, arrived safely in Tlaxcala.

Below *A scene from the* Noche Triste *(Sad Night), showing the Spaniards retreating in disarray from the capital.*

Taking the Capital

After three weeks' rest in Tlaxcala, Cortés once again ordered his battle-scarred troops into action. Supported by several thousand Tlaxcalans, they swept southward, subduing the people of Tepeaca who were Aztec allies. As many as 60,000 Tepeacans died; the survivors were taken as slaves.

The campaign gave Cortés control of the most direct route from the coast. He established a town, Segura de la Frontera, and remained there for some months. With the arrival of 200 soldiers from Jamaica, his forces now numbered about 600.

In a second lengthy letter to the Spanish king, Cortés recorded all that had happened, grandly calling himself "Captain-General of New Spain of the Ocean Sea." He went to much trouble to justify the system of slavery he was imposing: in a modified form, it was to remain in place for centuries.

At Tlaxcala, a fleet of thirteen brigantines was under construction for the forthcoming assault on the Aztec capital. The ships would have to be carried 50 mi (80 km) overland to the lake. Meanwhile, during the first months of 1521, Cortés pitched all his forces, which included at least 100,000 Indian allies, against the various lakeside cities. He occupied Texcoco, close to the eastern shore, and made it his base.

Below Much of the battle for Tenochtitlán was fought on water, as the Spaniards attempted to cut off the city's supply route.

One after another, the Aztec cities fell to the *conquistadores*. But the fighting took a heavy toll. During a fierce three-day battle for the town of Xochimilco, Cortés himself was very nearly captured. The Aztec ruler Cuitláhuac, like many other Indians, had died of smallpox – a disease brought to Mexico by the Spaniards. His successor was Cuauhtémoc who intended to resist the Spanish forces to the end.

By May, the Spanish ships were ready. Carried from Tlaxcala to Texcoco, they were launched into the lake along a specially built canal. Cortés divided his forces, now 900 strong, into four sections; with each went 40,000 warriors.

The battle for Tenochtitlán began on the causeways. There were barricades to cross and many gaps filled with underwater stakes. From rooftops and from canoes, Aztecs kept up a constant bombardment of the Spanish forces.

The fleet could do little against the canoes. Again Cortés himself was almost captured; many Spanish prisoners were sacrificed by the Aztecs in full view of their comrades. But gradually the Spanish progressed.

After sixty days and nights of battle, Cortés entered the city. The Aztecs resisted to the last. In the the battle, men, women and children were slaughtered by the thousand. Then at last, Cuauhtémoc was captured. It was August 13, 1521, and the end of the Aztec nation.

Ruling Passions

The first priority for Cortés was to rebuild the shattered city. The Indians worked furiously. The lake surrounding the city was largely filled with rubble; stones and timber were brought down from the mountains into the valley; and streets and squares were laid out in the Spanish style. Before long, a new capital, now known as Mexico City, was rising from the ruins of Tenochtitlán.

Thinking of the country's future development, Cortés sent out groups of explorers to find land suitable for farming. From Spain and the Indies, he imported breeding-stock (sheep, cattle, pigs, horses and poultry) together with grain, seeds and cuttings of various fruits and vegetables.

In some parts of the country, areas of Indian resistance still remained, but these were soon overcome. Cortés also had political rivals, but a long-delayed letter from the Spanish king confirmed him as Governor of Mexico, or "New Spain," in 1522.

His personal life was complicated by the arrival from Cuba of his wife, Catalina, who died shortly afterward in very suspicious circumstances; it looked to many people as though

Below Two Spanish cities of the New World: Mexico City (left) and Cuazc (right), formerly the Inca capital of Peru.

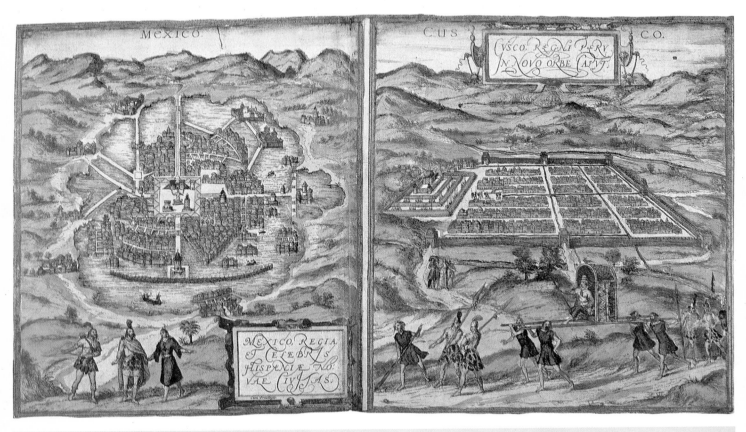

Left *An engraving showing the* conquistadores *ill-treating the defeated Mexicans.*

Cortés had poisoned her. By now, he had fathered children by several other women, including both Marina and a daughter of Montezuma. The union of Mexico and Spain was to result in a new people, the Mestizos.

Toward the end of 1523, Cortés turned to a new project: the search for an Atlantic-Pacific passageway, or sea-link. (In fact, until the building of the Panama Canal in 1904–14, no such link existed.) He sent out ships to explore each coast. Then, some months later, came unwelcome news. In faraway Honduras, the leader of an expedition had rebelled and set up his own small empire.

Cortés not only sent a force by sea to capture the rebel. To be doubly sure, he decided to march to Honduras himself, at the head of a large army. The march started in style, Cortés and Marina side by side, accompanied by many courtiers, and even some musicians and jugglers. Soon however, the journey turned into a nightmare.

There were swamps and rivers to cross. The soldiers had to build many bridges, some of which were very flimsy, while others were marvels of engineering. Sometimes, dense forests barred the way; there were also mountain passes edged by ravines.

Along the way, having had word of a plot, he ordered the execution of Cuauhtémoc, the last emperor of the Aztecs, who had been taken as a hostage. Even Cortés' own men thought this a cruel, unjust act. Finally, the march turned out to have been unnecessary. Reaching his goal, Cortés found that the rebel captain had been caught and killed already.

Homecoming

The march to Honduras had taken a whole year to complete, and it was another six months before Cortés returned by ship to Mexico. While he had been away, many disputes had broken out among the officials he had left to govern in his place. "New Spain" seemed close to chaos, and Cortés had formally been declared dead.

His return was for most people a cause for celebration. All the way from the coast to the capital, Cortés was greeted by joyful Indian crowds, offering gifts and scattering flowers before him. But he was never to regain his position of power.

An agent of the Spanish king arrived in Mexico to investigate the many complaints of misgovernment by Cortés, which had been made in the meantime by his rivals. It was a lengthy process and Cortés was deprived of his governorship. Eventually he decided to travel to Spain and present his case to the king.

He made the voyage in 1528. It was a spectacular homecoming. The great *conquistador* was accompanied by many of his comrades, and by various Indian nobles, including a son of Montezuma. There were also Indian acrobats, jugglers, dancers and other performers, together with a collection of strange and exotic beasts such as armadillos, ant-eaters, ocelots and opossums. Cortés brought a great deal of gold, silver, jewelry, several finely carved emerald statues, and superb feather cloaks and headdresses.

Below *At the court of King Charles, Cortés was welcomed. However, he did not consider that his rewards did justice to his achievements.*

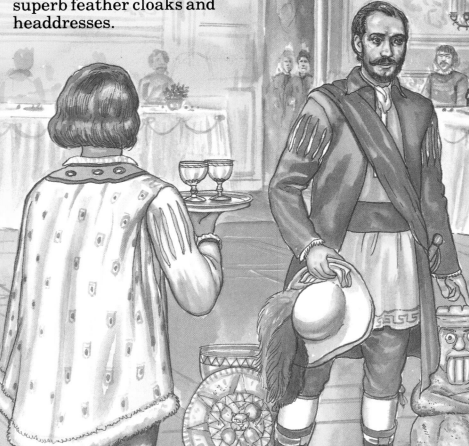

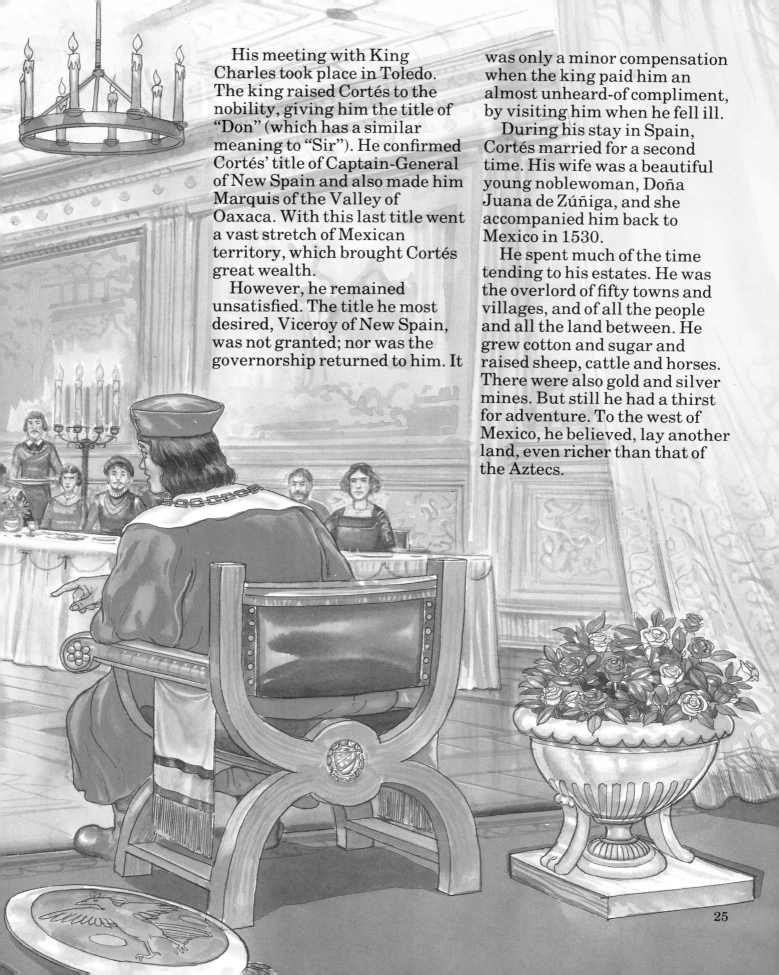

His meeting with King Charles took place in Toledo. The king raised Cortés to the nobility, giving him the title of "Don" (which has a similar meaning to "Sir"). He confirmed Cortés' title of Captain-General of New Spain and also made him Marquis of the Valley of Oaxaca. With this last title went a vast stretch of Mexican territory, which brought Cortés great wealth.

However, he remained unsatisfied. The title he most desired, Viceroy of New Spain, was not granted; nor was the governorship returned to him. It was only a minor compensation when the king paid him an almost unheard-of compliment, by visiting him when he fell ill.

During his stay in Spain, Cortés married for a second time. His wife was a beautiful young noblewoman, Doña Juana de Zúñiga, and she accompanied him back to Mexico in 1530.

He spent much of the time tending to his estates. He was the overlord of fifty towns and villages, and of all the people and all the land between. He grew cotton and sugar and raised sheep, cattle and horses. There were also gold and silver mines. But still he had a thirst for adventure. To the west of Mexico, he believed, lay another land, even richer than that of the Aztecs.

25

Soldiering On

Cíbola was a mythical kingdom, where cities were said to be built of gold. During his visit to Spain, Cortés learned that King Charles was eager that Cíbola be found, and he had agreed to share generously in any wealth it might provide. Cortés believed he could repeat his Mexican triumph and was determined to try.

He ordered ships to be built on the Pacific coast near modern-day Acapulco, and in 1532, the first two set out. One was never seen again, the other returned with nothing to report. In 1534 two more ships set sail, but they, too, were lost. Cortés decided he would command the next attempt.

He gathered together a force of more than 400 men, one hundred on horseback, and they marched nearly 620 mi (1,000 km) from Cuernavaca to the coast near Mazatlán. There, they met up with three ships from Acapulco, and in May 1535 the leading party, headed by Cortés, set out to sea.

Before long they reached the southern tip of Lower California. Cortés claimed the land for Spain and sent his ships back for the rest of his men. But only one ship returned; the others were lost. He set off in search of the ships and managed to find them, but the attempt as a whole seemed doomed to failure.

On the barren shore, his men nearly starved. The few Indian inhabitants had no knowledge of the mysterious Cíbola. Exploratory trips to the north brought no results. Three times Cortés crossed the gulf for extra supplies. Eventually, after

Above This seventeenth-century map, which is partly imaginary, shows the lands of South America that were conquered by the Spanish.

a year of fruitless effort, the exhausted travelers were glad to return to Mexico.

Once again, Cortés became caught up in political quarrels. He also wanted to make another attempt to find Cíbola, but the newly appointed viceroy refused him permission. In 1540 he left Mexico for Spain, intending, as before, to see the king. He was never to return.

When Cortés reached Spain, King Charles was away, fighting at the head of his army in The Netherlands. A year later the king rode south, to lead a massive force of men and ships against the Moorish city of Algiers. Cortés was among the Spanish volunteers for this mission, with two of his sons.

He had no chance to organize a meeting with the king.

When the fleet was ready to attack, a terrible storm broke, wrecking 150 ships. Cortés was one of the few shipwrecked survivors. He offered to lead a force of just 400 men against the city, and was laughed at. He was fifty-six years old. The king's generals had no time for him.

He tried again and again to put his case. A story was later told of how he once clung onto the king's carriage as it passed in the street. "Who is this man?" asked the royal occupant. "Sire," said Cortés, "I am the man who brought Your Majesty more kingdoms than you once had cities." The king drove on and Cortés was lost in the crowd.

Below *The coast of Baja (Lower) California was the location of Cortés' last expedition in the Americas.*

The Legacy of Cortés

The years of exploration and battle were over. They had taken their toll, in health and in wealth. Cortés died in December 1547, at the age of sixty-two, neglected by the court.

At the end of his life he had wanted to return to Mexico; and it was there that he wanted to be buried. For twenty years, his remains lay in a tomb in the Spanish city of Seville before they were finally taken to the land of his conquests.

By that time, the Spanish empire extended throughout the Americas; from what is now the western United States, through Central America, Colombia and Peru, to Chile and Argentina in the far south.

The most notable of the *conquistadores* to follow Cortés was probably Francisco Pizarro, who defeated and destroyed the great civilization of the Incas in Peru in the mid-1530s.

Spanish-American society was ordered and stable for many years. In Mexico, government officials from Spain formed the ruling class. Land was largely the property of people of pure Spanish descent who had been born in Mexico.

The Indians were forced to work on the lands of their Spanish masters. People of Spanish-Indian descent, the Mestizos, were usually town-dwellers. They formed Mexico's merchant class.

Gold and silver from Mexico helped to make Spain the world's most powerful nation in the sixteenth century. One of the original aims of the *conquistadores* was to find gold. The foot-soldiers of Cortés' army gained almost nothing, but Spain was richly rewarded.

The first missionary priests arrived soon after Cortés. In the following years, Catholicism

Far left *Francisco Pizzaro (c1478–1541), conqueror of Peru.*

Left *Hernan Cortés (1485–1547), conqueror of Mexico.*

swiftly replaced the local religions. The festivals, stories and dances of the region, however, still show many traces of former ways.

In the early years of the nineteenth century, Mexico gained its independence, as did Spain's other American colonies. So strong were the feelings in Mexico against Spain that the bones of Cortés were threatened with public burning. But when his tomb was broken into, it was found to be empty. His remains had been hidden away.

The twentieth century witnessed the last Mexican revolution, which freed the Indians from bondage. During this period, Catholicism was fiercely attacked, and some churches fell into disuse.

In 1947, in the church where they had originally lain, the remains of Cortés were rediscovered, bricked into a wall. They were reburied, and the church, which Cortés himself had founded in 1527, was restored. Loathed by some, admired by others, Hernan Cortés, like the other *conquistadoes*, remains a controversial figure.

Above *A beautifully detailed seventeenth-century painting of the central square of Mexico City.*

Glossary

Allegiance Official loyalty, often sworn on oath.

Armadillo Small mammal with an armor-like covering of bony plates.

Aviary A building housing captive birds.

Brigantine Small sailing ship, usually with two masts and square sails on the foremast.

Caravel Type of sailing ship originating in the Mediterranean, generally with two or three masts, usually used in coastal trade.

Citadel A castle-fortress in or near a city.

Colony A country governed by a foreign power.

Conquistador/Conquistadores (Spanish) Conqueror/Conquerers – specifically, soldiers who won the Americas for Spain, 1510–50.

Grant A "gift" from a government (or other organization), with conditions attached.

Missionary Priest or preacher who travels to foreign countries to spread religion.

Mestizo Someone of mixed European and Indian ancestry (from a Spanish word meaning "mixed").

Moors A Muslim people who invaded Spain in the eighth century.

Mosaic A patterned surface made of fragments of stone, glass, etc.

Muslim A believer in the religion of Islam.

Ocelot Yellowish-brown striped cat, related to the leopard.

Omen A sign of good or bad luck to come.

Opossum Tree-living animal of the marsupial family (its offspring are carried in the mother's pouch).

Psychological Having to do with the way that people's minds work.

Serfdom The system by which poor or unpaid workers are legally "tied" or bonded to land owned by someone else.

Tortilla A round, thin "pancake" made of cornmeal.

Books to Read

The Age of Exploration by Alan Blackwood (Bookwright, 1990)

Aztecs by Jill Hughes (Gloucester, 1986)

Aztecs by Barbara L. Beck (Franklin Watts, 1983)

Aztecs and Incas by Penny Bateman (Franklin Watts, 1988)

Mexican Food and Drink by Manuel Alvarado (Bookwright, 1988)

Mexico by Sam & Beryl Epstein (Franklin Watts, 1983)

Montezuma and the Aztecs by Nathaniel Harris (Bookwright, 1986)

We Live in Mexico by Carlos Somonte (Bookwright, 1985)

Picture Acknowledgments

The publishers would like to thank the following for their illustrations: Bridgeman Art Library 5 (bottom), 11 (top), 22, 26, 29; E.T. Archive 6 (bottom); The Mansell Collection *frontispiece*; Mary Evans 6 (top), 7 (top), 18, 19; Peter Newark's Western Americana 4, 10, 23; Photri 11 (bottom), 28 (both); Tony Stone Picture Library 4 (top), 7 (bottom), 27. All maps are by Peter Bull.

Finding out More

In the Spanish conquest of America, whole civilizations and ways of life were wiped out. With them went most of the buildings, objects and literature these people had produced – their day-to-day business accounts, as well as their precious books of knowledge and religion; their everyday craftwork, as well as their palaces and sacred statues. Unique objects of gold and silver were melted down for the value of their metal.

Consequently, museums often have little to show of the Aztec period.

If you travel to Spain you will be able to see museum collections devoted to the *conquistadores*: their arms and armor, their maps and manuscripts, their personal possessions. Travel to Mexico and you can see the ruined sites of the Aztecs and their neighbors, and the kind of terrain that Cortés had to cross.

Index